My Little Red Book Of Wisdoms

(Inspirational quotes from my 13 year-old self)

By

Leila Khan

Life Is Today Life Coaching and Publishing

20-23 Woodside Place

Glasgow

G3 7QF

UK

www.litlifecoaching.com

About The Author

Leila Khan is certified Neuro-Linguistic Programming Practitioner, transformational life coach and self-published author. She works with clients who want to eliminate fears, worries and negative thinking patterns, through coaching and hypnosis, so that they feel happy, motivated and inspired to achieve their dreams and goals. She also offers motivational talks, workshops and speaking engagements on topics such as NLP, self-esteem and confidence, overcoming hardships and living a brave and courageous life. She started to put this collection of quotes together when she was 13 years old and hopes to pass on the uplifting quotes to others who are seeking some guidance and inspiration. Pick it up, read a quote and feel inspired!

Her website is www.litlifecoaching.com

INTRODUCTION

Letter to my 13 year old self:

You've made it my darling, your dream has come true! Here's your book, the one that you started to write when you were only 13 years old. You have made it! You have found what happiness means, you have exercised courage, you have stayed true to yourself and you have stood up and been counted. More than anything, I know how much you wanted to make your life matter and overcome all the hard stuff. Here it is my little Angel, you matter. Your life has mattered and you are helping so many people in this world to heal, to love themselves first and be true to who they are. Your heartbeats count

xxx

Take nothing for granted,
always be grateful.
Leila Khan

Never apologise for who you are.
Unknown

*I always prefer to believe
the best in everybody,
it saves so much time.*
Rudyard Kipling

*You are not responsible
for anyone else's feelings.*
Unknown

If it is be, it is up to me.
Unknown

*La plus grande chose du monde,
c'est de savoir être à soi. (The
greatest thing in the world is to
know how to be one's own.)*
Michel De Montaigne

The golden rule is that there are no golden rules.

George Bernard Shaw

Never judge a book by its cover.
Unknown

It's not what you say but how you say it that makes all the difference.

Unknown

Do not follow where the path may lead. Go instead where there is no path and leave a trail.

Ralph Waldo Emerson

*No one can ever make you feel
inferior without your consent.*
Eleanor Roosevelt

Use what talents you possess.
The woods would be very silent
if no birds sang there
except those that sang best.
Henry Van Dyke

The kid in you never dies.
Leila Khan

Be a chancer, not a quitter.
Leila Khan

*You can always do better
than your best.*
Leila Khan

Live your life, don't let life live you.

Leila Khan

Once something is said and done,
there is nothing you can do
about it. So speak kindly
in the first place.
Leila Khan

Everyone has their own merits.
Leila Khan

Kind words can be short and easy to speak but their echoes are truly endless.
Mother Theresa

Children have more need of
models than critics.
Joseph Joubert

Life is a bundle of hurdles.
Leila Khan

Tout comprendre rend très indulgent.
(To be totally understanding
makes one very indulgent.)
Germaine de Staël

You are your own greatest asset-there is nothing you cannot do. No one can keep you from dreaming your dreams and only you can prevent them from coming true.

Your achievements are not determined by your ability alone, but by the desire you possess to reach them. There are no worlds outside of those you create for yourself, and the only boundaries are those you establish and choose to live within. Never be afraid to defend your decision, regardless.
No one can possibly know what is best for other than yourself.

Terry Everton

30

It's better to have been
a has-been, than a never was.
Unknown

Don't let others' stupidity get you down.
Unknown

Somebody's faith gives
another courage to fly.
Leila Khan

There are no boundaries apart from those you set yourself.
Leila Khan

While an original is always hard to find, he is easy to recognise.
John L. Mason

Don't be afraid to be friendly.
Unknown

*If you fall off the saddle
get back on the horse.*
Unknown

You cannot discover new oceans unless you have the courage to lose sight of the shore.
André Gide

Courage is very important, like a muscle it is strengthened by use.
Ruth Gordon

The sky's the limit if you let it be.
Unknown

Fortune favours the brave.
Unknown

*The sky's the limit
if your heart is in it.*
Unknown

*Take the bull by
its horns and go for it.*
Unknown

There is no point in
dwelling in the past.
Leila Khan

There is no such thing as can't.
Leila Khan

Do what you want not what everybody else wants you to do.
Leila Khan

When there's a will there's a way.
Old English Proverb

Work smart, not hard.
Unknown

You must do the things
you think you cannot do.
Leila Khan

*Don't be afraid of the
things you can't do or you'll
always be scared.*
Leila Khan

When the old times go, let them go. If someone has died let them go, but just make sure they never die in your heart.

Leila Khan

Time is what you make of it.
Unknown

No time like the present.
Unknown

The future has a way
of arriving unannounced.
George Will

Youth which is forgiven everything, forgives itself nothing. Age which forgives itself anything is forgiven nothing.

George Bernard Shaw

My advice is to never do tomorrow what you can do today. Procrastination is the thief of time.

Charles Dickens

*Go back and read
what you wrote.*
Jerry Maguire

Men talk of killing, when time is quietly killing them.

Dion Boucicault

Only when the day approaches do you really begin to care.

Unknown

The past holds us down,
the future worries us and so we
miss the present.
Unknown

Whatever goes around,
comes around.
Unknown

If the sky is dull and grey, don't let it spoil your day.
A friend

The word impossible is not in my dictionary.
Napoleon Bonaparte

*Dream dreams no one
else can see, then one day
show them to your friends.*
Leila Khan

*Champions keep playing until
they get it right.*
Billie Jean King

*Reality is something you
have to rise above.*
Liza Minnelli

There is always room at the top.
Daniel Webster

A man's reach should not
exceed his grasp. Or else,
what's a heaven for?
    Robert Browning,
    Men and women
    and Other Poems

The sky's your limit
if you let it be.
   Unknown

*If you think of nothing but
what you want to be,
then one day you will be it.*
Whoopi Goldberg
Sister Act

Aim high and never settle for second best.
School teacher

The key to happiness is having dreams. The key to success is making dreams come true.
James Allen

Some people dream of worthy accomplishments while others stay awake and do them.
Unknown

*Absence makes the
heart grow fonder.*
**(The contemporary version appears
in The Pocket Magazine of Classic
and Polite Literature, 1832, in a piece
by a Miss Stickland)**

No one can predict to what heights you will soar, even you will not know until you spread your wings.

Whoopi Goldberg

*There are two tragedies in life;
one is not to get your heart's desire.
The other is to get it.*
George Bernard Shaw

Don't be afraid to fly,
spread your wings.
Unknown

Opportunity will always involve some risks. You can't steal second base and keep your foot on the first.
Frederick B Wilcox

Find a job you love and
you'll never have to work again.
Confucius

Teaching kids what to do is fine,
but teaching them
what counts is best.
Bob Talbert

Comments are free
but facts are sacred.
C.P. Scott

He who can does,
he who cannot, teaches.
George Bernard Shaw

Education is what survives when what has been learnt has been forgotten.
B.F. Skinner

*The heart has its reasons which
reason knows nothing of...
We know the truth not only
by the reason, but by the heart.*
Blaise Pascal

Reading is to the mind what exercise is to the body.
Joseph Addison

*If we do not find anything
pleasant, at least we
shall find something new.*
Voltaire

The man who makes no mistakes
does not usually make anything.
Edward John Phelps

The more alternatives, the more difficult the choice.

Abbe' D'Allanival

*The way to be a bore
is to tell everything.*
Voltaire

*A good teacher is a
teacher never forgotten.*
Unknown

*Great minds think alike
but fools seldom differ.*
English proverb

If you think you can, you can. If you think you can't, you're right.
Henry Ford

Genius does what it must and talent does what it can.
Edward George Bulwer- Lytton

They are the richest whose pleasures are the cheapest.
David Henry Thoreau

A wise man will make more opportunities than he finds.

Francis Bacon

Your life is your movie so don't let others take the lead role.
A friend

Whatever will be will be.
Doris Day

The true paradises are the paradises we have lost.
Marcel Proust

The best things in life are free.
Luther Vandross &
Janet Jackson

*Better by far you should forget
and smile, than that you should
remember and be sad.*

Christina Rossetti

*A place for everything and
everything in its place.*
Benjamin Franklin

If you want a rainbow you've got to have the rain.

Dolly Parton

*It's your life so don't
let others run it for you.*
Leila Khan

*Tout est pour le mieux dans le
meilleur des mondes.
(All is for the best in the best of
all possible worlds.)*
Voltaire

Life is what you make it.
Unknown

Experience is the name so many people give their mistakes.
Oscar Wilde

May all your troubles last as long as your New Year's resolutions.
Joey Adams

*It's a funny thing about life; if
you refuse to accept anything but
the best, you very often get it.*
W. Somerset Maugham

Life is full of compromises and defeats with few victories to show for it.

Zora Neale Hurston
Seraph on the Suwanee

*Life is ours to be
spent not to be saved.*
D.H. Lawrence

Miracles happen to those who believe in them.

Bernard Berenson

You will always miss 100% of
the shots you don't take.
Wayne Gretzky

*Difficult is the excuse
history never accepts.*
        Edward R. Murrow

The secret of happiness is to admire without desiring.
F. H. Bradley

Success is getting what you want, happiness is liking what you've got.

H. Jackson Brown, Jr

We can't direct the wind, but we can adjust the sails. For maximum happiness, peace, and contentment, may we choose a positive attitude.

Thomas S. Monson

Less is more.
Andrea del Sarto

There is a superstition in avoiding superstition.
Francis Bacon

Silence is the virtue of fools.
Francis Bacon

*The remedy is worse
than the disease.*
Francis Bacon

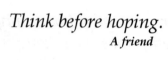

Think before hoping.
A friend

Your mind might be empty but emptiness is a thought.
A friend

*Obstacles are those things
you see when you take your eyes
off the goals.*
Henry Ford

A friend is someone who walks in when the world walks out.
Walter Winchell

*A friend is a lot of things
but a critic he isn't.*
Bernard Williams

*Treat your friends as you do
your pictures, place them
in the best light.*

Jennie Jerome Churchill
Mother of Winston Churchill

*It is with narrow-souled people
as with narrow necked bottles;
the less they have in them
the more noise they make in
pouring it out.*
Alexander Wise

127

Curiosity killed the cat.
The Galveston Daily News, 1898

A friend is a person who tells you all the nice things you always knew about yourself.
Unknown

Friendship is far more delicate than love.
Oscar Wilde

From the rocking horse to the rocking chair, friendship keeps teaching us about being human.
Letty Cottin Pogrebin

The best mirror is an old friend.
George Herbert

It takes a long time to
grow an old friend.
John Leonard

Sometimes being a friend means mastering the art of timing. There is a time for silence. A time to let go and allow people to hurl themselves into their own destiny. And a time to prepare to pick up the pieces when it's all over.

Gloria Naylor

May the road run with the wind always at your back and may God hold you in the hollow of his hand.

Irish blessing

Sometimes the worst times are the times when you need a friend the most.

Leila Khan

I'd rather be a failure at something I enjoy, than be a success at something I hate.

George Burns

There are no shortcuts to any place worth going.
Beverley Sills

You can't put a price tag on love
but you can on all it's accessories.
Melanie Clark

I can no longer remain as I was...
you have led me to the
sunny side where growth is a
matter of course.

Unknown

The man who speaks the truth is always at ease.

Persian Proverb

Winners never quit,
quitters never win.
Vince Lombardi

You cannot hold back a good laugh anymore than you can hold back the tide. Both are forces of nature.

William Rotsler

Nothing is so embarrassing as watching someone do something you said couldn't be done.

Sam Ewing

The truth of the matter is that you always know what the right thing is to do. The hard part is doing it.

Norman Schwarzkopf

*The average tourist wants to go
to places where
there are no tourists.*
Sam Ewing

If a window of opportunity appears, don't pull down the shade.
Tom Peters

It is better to have tried and
failed, than to not
have tried at all.
                    Unknown

There is nothing either good or bad, but thinking makes it so.
William Shakespeare

You become what you believe.
Oprah Winfrey

When one door closes, another one opens.
Alexander Graham Bell

Real friends have no problem with silence.

Leila Khan

And what is laughter anyway?
Changing the angle of vision.
That is what you love a friend
for: the ability to change your
angle of vision, bring back your
best self when you feel worst,
remind you of your strengths
when you feel weak.

Erica Jong

No love, no friendship, can cross the path of our destiny without leaving some mark on it forever.
François Mauriac

Friendship doubles our joy and divides our grief.
Swedish Proverb

I hope you feel inspired to know that you have all the courage, faith and strength within you to experience your full potential.

Leila
December 2013